Checks Mix Quilts

Get the Gingham Look You Love
with 8 Easy-to-Piece Patterns

Corey Yoder

Martingale®
Create with Confidence

Checks Mix Quilts: Get the Gingham Look You Love with
8 Easy-to-Piece Patterns
© 2020 by Corey Yoder

Martingale®
18939 120th Ave. NE, Ste. 101
Bothell, WA 98011-9511 USA
ShopMartingale.com

Printed in Hong Kong
25 24 23 22 21   8 7 6 5 4 3 2

Library of Congress Cataloging-in-Publication Data is available upon request.

ISBN: 978-1-68356-108-8

MISSION STATEMENT

We empower makers who use fabric and yarn to make life more enjoyable.

CREDITS

PUBLISHER AND
CHIEF VISIONARY OFFICER
Jennifer Erbe Keltner

CONTENT DIRECTOR
Karen Costello Soltys

DESIGN MANAGER
Adrienne Smitke

MANAGING EDITOR
Tina Cook

PRODUCTION MANAGER
Regina Girard

ACQUISITIONS AND
DEVELOPMENT EDITOR
Laurie Baker

COVER AND
BOOK DESIGNER
Mia Mar

TECHNICAL EDITOR
Carolyn Beam

PHOTOGRAPHERS
Adam Albright
Brent Kane

COPY EDITOR
Durby Peterson

ILLUSTRATOR
Sandy Loi

SPECIAL THANKS
*Photography for this book was taken at the homes
of Libby Warnken of Ankeny, Iowa, and
Tracie Fish of Kenmore, Washington.*

contents

introduction

A few years ago, I designed a Christmas quilt for a Moda All-Stars book, *Merry Makers: Patchwork Quilts and Projects to Celebrate the Season* (Martingale, 2018). The pattern was called Merry Gingham Lap Quilt, and it featured strip-pieced sections of fabrics in a gingham design. Not long after that, I incorporated a similar gingham into a new quilt pattern I was releasing called Gingham Garden, a design that included strips of pieced gingham set amid a garden of flowers.

Both quilts got me thinking about all of the fun ways gingham could be added to quilts. And thus, the idea for *Checks Mix Quilts* was born.

Each quilt features a pieced check of some sort. Some of the checks are large and some are small. Even the smaller checks become simple to make with the help of strip piecing. And trust me, they're a whole lot more fun than the checks we write to pay bills!

I use a striped fabric for the binding on nearly all of my quilts. Because I like striped binding so much, I include a different stripe in each fabric collection I design. I've listed the fabric collection for each binding fabric I used in these projects, just in case you love striped binding too.

The quilts within these pages span the seasons. You'll find projects to fill your home for any time of the year. From snowmen to hearts, flags, and leaves, you might find yourself "checking" these quilts off of your to-do list sooner rather than later.

Happy sewing!

Corey

check your heart

Choosing fabrics is one of my favorite parts of quiltmaking. If you're intimidated by that part of the process, Check Your Heart is the quilt for you. You need only two prints, so picking the fabrics is a breeze. The trickiest part is narrowing it down to just two!

finished quilt: 46½" × 58½"
finished blocks: 6" × 6"

materials

Yardage is based on 42"-wide fabric. Fabrics for the quilt top are from Nest by Lella Boutique, and binding fabric is from my Sugarcreek collection, all from Moda Fabrics.

1⅓ yards of light pink print for blocks

⅞ yard of dark pink print for blocks

1⅞ yards of white solid for block backgrounds

½ yard of dark pink stripe for binding

3⅛ yards of fabric for backing

55" × 67" piece of batting

choosing fabrics

Select a dark and a light print of the same color to create the checked effect. Choose a contrasting solid for the background, which will play a fun part in the design. Each heart appears to be cut out of the print that surrounds it.

check your heart

Designed by Corey Yoder
Pieced by Stephanie Crabtree
Quilted by Kaylene Parry

- - - -

cutting

All measurements include ¼"-wide seam allowances.

From the light pink print, cut:

4 strips, 2½" × 42"; crosscut into 62 squares, 2½" × 2½"

19 strips, 1½" × 42"; crosscut into:
- 62 rectangles, 1½" × 6½"
- 62 rectangles, 1½" × 4½"

4 strips, 1" × 42"; crosscut into 124 squares, 1" × 1"

From the dark pink print, cut:

3 strips, 2½" × 42"; crosscut into 40 squares, 2½" × 2½"

12 strips, 1½" × 42"; crosscut into:
- 40 rectangles, 1½" × 6½"
- 40 rectangles, 1½" × 4½"

2 strips, 1" × 42"; crosscut into 80 squares, 1" × 1"

From the white solid, cut:

2 strips, 6½" × 42"; crosscut into 12 squares, 6½" × 6½"

19 strips, 2½" × 42"; crosscut *13 of the strips* into 102 rectangles, 2½" × 4½"

From the dark pink stripe, cut:

6 strips, 2½" × 42"

binding width

Although the cutting list calls for standard 2½"-wide binding strips, I frequently cut my binding strips only 2" wide because I machine bind my quilts, first sewing the binding to the back and then bringing it to the front and topstitching. I find that a narrower binding allows me greater accuracy when stitching the binding in place.

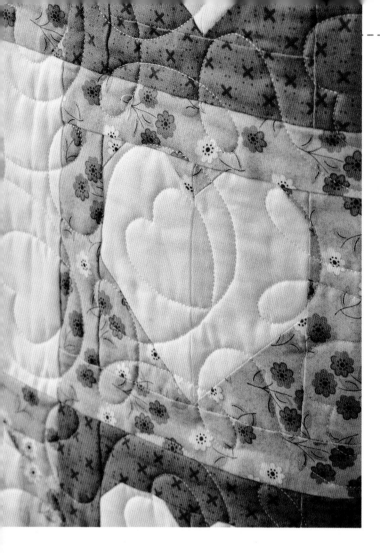

the rectangle. Repeat to make a total of 62 units measuring 2½" × 4½", including seam allowances.

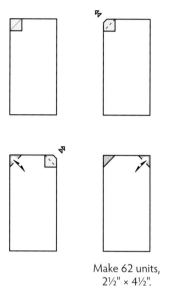

Make 62 units,
2½" × 4½".

3 Place a marked light pink 2½" square on the bottom of a step 2 unit, right sides together. Sew on the marked line. Trim the excess corner fabric, leaving a ¼" seam allowance. Repeat to make a total of 31 left heart units measuring 2½" × 4½", including seam allowances.

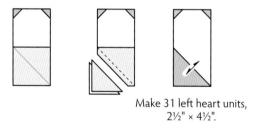

Make 31 left heart units,
2½" × 4½".

4 Repeat step 3 with the remaining step 2 units and marked light pink 2½" squares, orienting the squares as shown, to make 31 right heart units measuring 2½" × 4½", including seam allowances.

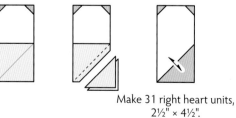

Make 31 right heart units,
2½" × 4½".

making the blocks

Press all seam allowances as indicated by the arrows.

1 Draw a diagonal line from corner to corner on the wrong side of each light pink and dark pink 1" square and each light pink and dark pink 2½" square.

2 Place a marked light pink 1" square on the upper-left corner of a white 2½" × 4½" rectangle, right sides together. Sew on the marked line. Trim the excess corner fabric, leaving a ¼" seam allowance. Repeat on the upper-right corner of

5 Sew each left heart unit to a right heart unit to make 31 heart units measuring 4½" square, including seam allowances.

Make 31 heart units,
4½" × 4½".

6 Sew light pink 1½" × 4½" rectangles to the sides of a heart unit. Sew light pink 1½" × 6½" rectangles to the top and bottom of the unit. Repeat to make a total of 31 light pink blocks measuring 6½" square, including seam allowances.

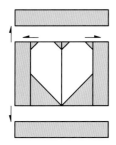

Make 31 light pink blocks,
6½" × 6½".

7 Repeat steps 2–5 with the dark pink squares to make a total of 20 dark pink heart units. Sew dark pink 1½" × 4½" rectangles to the top and bottom of a unit. Sew dark pink 1½" × 6½" rectangles to the sides of the unit. Repeat to make a total of 20 dark pink blocks measuring 6½" square, including seam allowances.

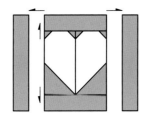

Make 20 dark pink blocks,
6½" × 6½".

assembling the quilt top

1 Refer to the quilt assembly diagram below to arrange the pieced blocks and white 6½" squares in nine horizontal rows. Sew together the blocks and squares in each row. Join the rows. The quilt top should measure 42½" × 54½", including seam allowances.

2 Join the remaining six white 2½" × 42" strips end to end to make one long strip. From the pieced strip, cut two strips, 2½" × 54½". Sew these strips to the sides of the quilt top. From the remainder of the pieced strip, cut two strips, 2½" × 46½". Sew these strips to the top and bottom of the quilt top. The completed quilt top should measure 46½" × 58½".

finishing the quilt

For help with any of the finishing steps, go to ShopMartingale.com/HowtoQuilt.

1 Layer the backing, batting, and quilt top; baste the layers together.

2 Hand or machine quilt as desired. The quilt shown is machine quilted with an allover pattern of hearts and loops using the Ginger Heart pantograph by Apricot Moon Designs.

3 Trim the excess batting and backing. Use the dark pink stripe 2½"-wide strips to make the binding. Attach the binding to the quilt.

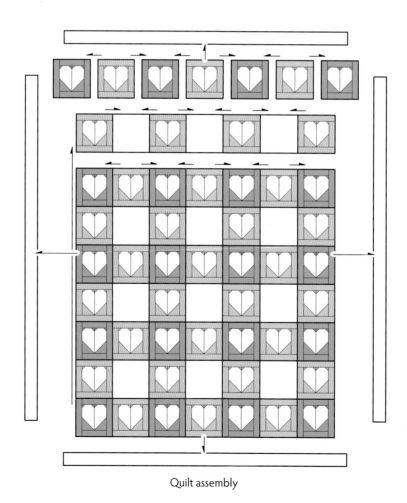

Quilt assembly

rain check

Initially, I planned to make a rainbow of spring flowers for Rain Check. But as I started playing with the fabrics, I fell in love with this sunflower version and its sunny yellows. What colors will bloom in *your* quilted garden?

finished quilt: 45½" × 54½"
finished blocks: 9" × 9"

materials

Yardage is based on 42"-wide fabric. Fabrics for the quilt top are from my various collections, and binding fabric is from my Sugarcreek Wovens collection, all from Moda Fabrics.

⅓ yard of dark gray print for block centers

⅓ yard of light gray print for block centers

2½ yards of white solid for block centers and background

⅛ yard *each* of 13 assorted yellow prints for blocks

⅓ yard of green print for flower stems and leaves

½ yard of gray stripe for binding

3 yards of fabric for backing

52" × 61" piece of batting

choosing fabrics

When selecting fabrics for the sunflower centers, choose a dark and a light shade of the same color. For the petals, keep in mind that warm colors will appear to advance and cool colors will appear to recede, so play around with color and see how you want the petals to flutter!

cutting

All measurements include ¼"-wide seam allowances.

From the dark gray print, cut:

6 strips, 1½" × 42"

From the light gray print, cut:

7 strips, 1½" × 42"

From the white solid, cut:

1 strip, 9½" × 42"; crosscut into 4 squares,
   9½" × 9½"

7 strips, 4" × 42"; crosscut into 52 rectangles,
   4" × 4¾"

4 strips, 2½" × 42"; crosscut into 52 squares,
   2½" × 2½"

2 strips, 2¼" × 42"; crosscut into 26 rectangles,
   2¼" × 2½"

14 strips, 1½" × 42"; crosscut *12 of the strips* into
   312 squares, 1½" × 1½"

7 strips, 1" × 42"; crosscut into 260 squares,
   1" × 1"

From *each* yellow print, cut:

8 rectangles, 2½" × 3" (104 total)

From the green print, cut:

2 strips, 2½" × 42"; crosscut into 26 rectangles,
   2½" × 3"

4 strips, 1" × 42"; crosscut into 13 rectangles,
   1" × 9½"

From the gray stripe, cut:

6 strips, 2½" × 42"

ruler to the rescue!

I love using the Creative Grids
Stripology ruler when I need a large
number of same-size squares. The
ruler saves so much time. You can cut
several strips at once and then turn
the ruler perpendicular to the cut lines
to cut squares from the strips.

making the flower blocks

Press all seam allowances as indicated by
the arrows.

1 Sew together three dark gray 1½" × 42"
strips and two light gray 1½" × 42" strips to
make strip set A. Make two strip sets. Crosscut
the strip sets into 39 A segments measuring
1½" × 5½", including seam allowances.

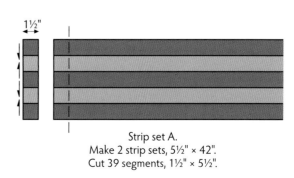

Strip set A.
Make 2 strip sets, 5½" × 42".
Cut 39 segments, 1½" × 5½".

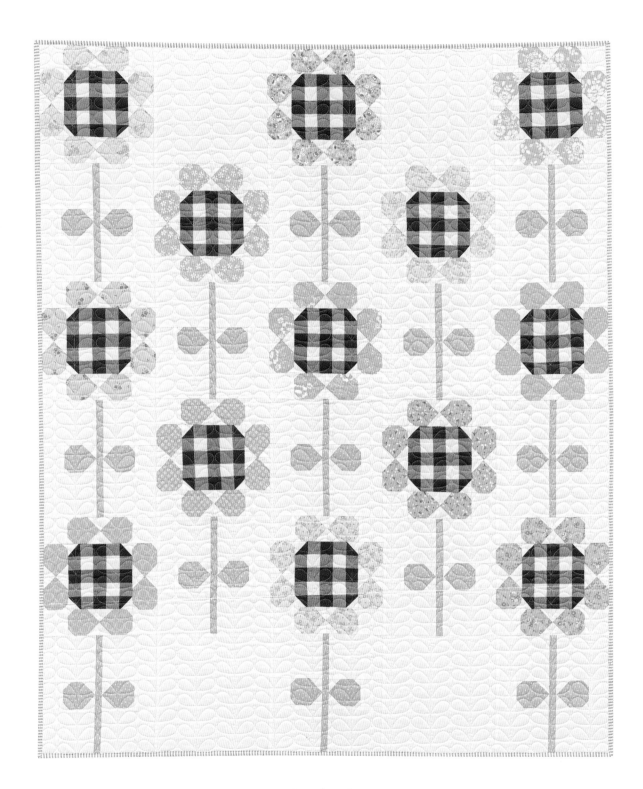

rain check

Designed by Corey Yoder
Pieced by Shannon Arnstein
Quilted by Kaylene Parry

- - - -

2 Repeat step 1 using three light gray 1½" × 42" strips and two white 1½" × 42" strips to make strip set B. Crosscut the strip set into 26 B segments measuring 1½" × 5½", including seam allowances.

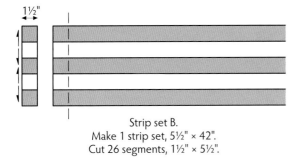

1½"

Strip set B.
Make 1 strip set, 5½" × 42".
Cut 26 segments, 1½" × 5½".

3 Sew together three A segments and two B segments as shown. Repeat to make a total of 13 flower-center units measuring 5½" square, including seam allowances.

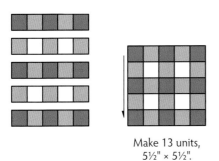

Make 13 units,
5½" × 5½".

4 Draw a diagonal line from corner to corner on the wrong side of 52 white 1½" squares. Place a marked square on the upper-left corner of a flower-center unit, right sides together. Sew on the marked line. Trim the excess corner fabric, leaving a ¼" seam allowance. Repeat on the remaining corners. Make 13 flower centers measuring 5½" square, including seam allowances.

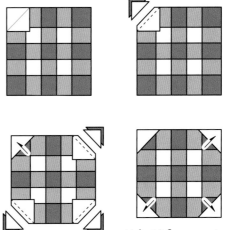

Make 13 flower centers,
5½" × 5½".

5 Draw a diagonal line from corner to corner on the wrong side of 208 white 1½" squares. Place a marked square on the upper-right corner of a yellow 2½" × 3" rectangle, right sides together. Sew on the marked line. Trim the excess corner fabric, leaving a ¼" seam allowance. Repeat on the lower-right corner, orienting the line as shown. Repeat to make a total of 104 units measuring 2½" × 3", including seam allowances.

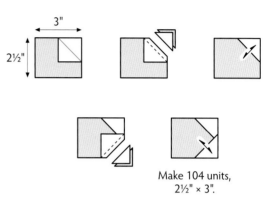

Make 104 units,
2½" × 3".

6 Draw a diagonal line from corner to corner on the wrong side of 208 white 1" squares. Place a marked square on the upper-left corner of a step 5 unit, right sides together. Sew on the marked line. Trim the excess corner fabric, leaving a ¼" seam allowance. Repeat on the lower-left corner, orienting the line as shown. Repeat to make a total of 104 petal units measuring 2½" × 3", including seam allowances.

Make 104 units,
2½" × 3".

7 Sew together two matching petals. Repeat to make a total of 52 matching petal pairs measuring 2½" × 5½", including seam allowances.

Make 52 pairs,
2½" × 5½".

8 Arrange a flower center, four matching petal pairs, and four white 2½" squares in three rows. Sew together the pieces in each row. Join the rows to complete the Flower block. Repeat to make a total of 13 Flower blocks measuring 9½" square, including seam allowances.

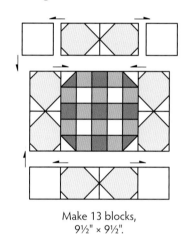

Make 13 blocks,
9½" × 9½".

making the stem blocks

1 The leaves on the Stem blocks are constructed in the same way as the petals of the Flower blocks. Follow steps 5–6 in "Making the Flower Blocks" to make each leaf. Substitute green 2½" × 3" rectangles for the yellow rectangles. Make a total of 26 leaves measuring 2½" × 3", including seam allowances.

Make 26 leaves,
2½" × 3".

2 Sew a white 2¼" × 2½" rectangle to the left edge of a leaf. Sew white 4" × 4¾" rectangles to the top and bottom to make a leaf unit. Repeat to make a total of 26 leaf units measuring 4¾" × 9½", including seam allowances.

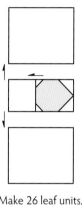

Make 26 leaf units,
4¾" × 9½".

3 Sew a leaf unit to each side of a green 1" × 9½" rectangle to make a Stem block. Repeat to make a total of 13 Stem blocks measuring 9½" square, including seam allowances.

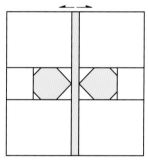

Make 13 blocks,
9½" × 9½".

assembling the quilt top

Refer to the quilt assembly diagram below to arrange the blocks and white 9½" squares in five vertical columns. Sew together the blocks and squares in each column. Join the columns. The quilt top should measure 45½" × 54½".

finishing the quilt

For help with any of the finishing steps, go to ShopMartingale.com/HowtoQuilt.

1 Layer the backing, batting, and quilt top; baste the layers together. Hand or machine quilt as desired. The quilt shown is machine quilted with an allover pattern of petals and stems using the 60s Mod quilting design by Julie Hirt.

2 Trim the excess batting and backing. Use the gray stripe 2½"-wide strips to prepare the binding. Attach the binding to the quilt.

Quilt assembly

Tossed checkerboard

Use strip piecing to make a super scrappy quilt that comes together quickly! Tossed Checkerboard is a great pattern for using up leftover 2½" strips you may have accumulated. Pair dark and light prints in each of seven different colorways for a delightfully colorful quilt.

finished quilt: 60½" × 75½"
finished blocks: 15" × 15"

materials

Yardage is based on 42"-wide fabric. Fabrics for the quilt top are from my various collections, and the binding fabric is from my Sunnyside Up collection, all from Moda Fabrics.

⅛ yard *each* of 20 assorted dark prints for blocks

¼ yard *each* of 20 assorted light prints for blocks

2½ yards of white solid for background

⅝ yard of rainbow stripe for binding

4¾ yards of fabric for backing

69" × 84" piece of batting

choosing fabrics

I selected the fabrics for these blocks in two different ways. For some blocks, I chose a light and a dark fabric of the same color. For other blocks, I picked the darker print first and then found a fabric with a white background that had a motif in the same color as the darker print.

cutting

All measurements include ¼"-wide seam allowances.

From *each* dark print, cut:

1 strip, 2½" × 42"; crosscut into 3 rectangles, 2½" × 12" (60 total)

From *each* light print, cut:

2 strips, 2½" × 42"; crosscut into:
- 2 rectangles, 2½" × 12" (40 total)
- 3 rectangles, 2½" × 8" (60 total)

From the white solid, cut:

20 strips, 3" × 42"; crosscut into 40 rectangles, 3" × 15½"

8 strips, 2½" × 42"; crosscut into 40 rectangles, 2½" × 8"

From the rainbow stripe, cut:

8 strips, 2½" × 42"

making the blocks

Press all seam allowances as indicated by the arrows. The instructions are written for making one block at a time. For each block, choose the rectangles cut from one dark and one light print of the same color.

1 Sew together three dark 2½" × 12" rectangles and two light 2½" × 12" rectangles, alternating the prints to make strip set A. Crosscut the strip set into three segments measuring 3½" × 10½", including seam allowances.

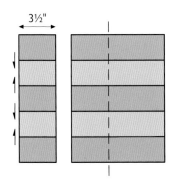

Strip set A.
Make 1 strip set, 10½" × 12".
Cut 3 segments, 3½" × 10½".

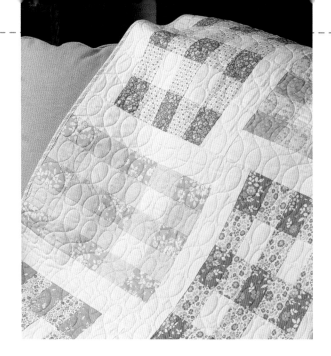

2 Repeat step 1 using three light 2½" × 8" rectangles and two white 2½" × 8" rectangles to make strip set B. Crosscut the strip set into two segments measuring 3½" × 10½", including seam allowances.

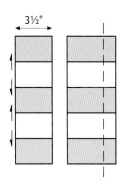

Strip set B.
Make 1 strip set, 10½" × 8".
Cut 2 segments, 3½" × 10½".

3 Sew together the A and B segments as shown to make a unit measuring 10½" × 15½", including seam allowances.

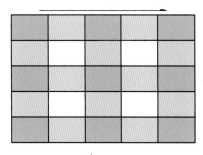

Make 1 unit,
10½" × 15½".

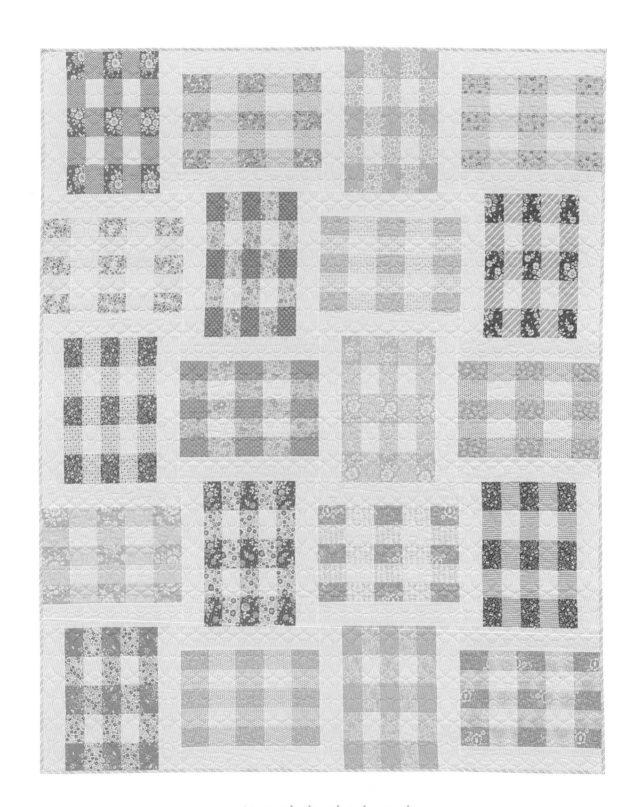

tossed checkerboard

Designed by Corey Yoder
Pieced by Natalie Crabtree
Quilted by Kaylene Parry

- - - -

4 Sew white 3" × 15½" rectangles to the top and bottom of the unit to make a block that measures 15½" square, including the seam allowances. Repeat all steps to make a total of 20 blocks.

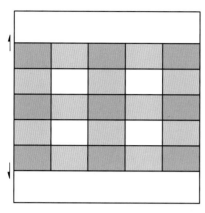

Make 20 blocks,
15½" × 15½".

assembling the quilt top

Refer to the quilt assembly diagram below to arrange the blocks in five horizontal rows of four blocks each, rotating the blocks as shown. Sew together the blocks in each row. Join the rows. The quilt top should measure 60½" × 75½".

finishing the quilt

For help with any of the finishing steps, go to ShopMartingale.com/HowtoQuilt.

1 Layer the backing, batting, and quilt top; baste the layers together. Hand or machine quilt as desired. The quilt shown is machine quilted with an allover pattern of loops using the Modern Loops quilting design by Anita Shackelford.

2 Trim the excess batting and backing. Use the rainbow stripe 2½"-wide strips to make the binding. Attach the binding to the quilt.

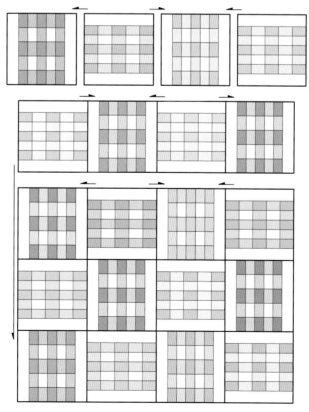

Quilt assembly

checkered flag

If you've ever been hesitant to try a quilt pattern with points, you can check your fears at the door! You'll enjoy each star you stitch in Checkered Flag. The technique used for the hourglass portion of the stars allows you to trim as you go, which makes piecing them a breeze.

finished quilt: 57½" × 57½"
finished blocks: 15" × 15"

materials

Yardage is based on 42"-wide fabric. Fat eighths measure 9" × 21". Fabrics for the quilt top are from my various collections, and binding fabric is from my Sugarcreek collection, all from Moda Fabrics.

⅞ yard of red print for blocks

⅝ yard of white-and-red print for blocks

3 yards of white solid for blocks and sashing

5 fat eighths (or scraps) of assorted blue prints for stars

¾ yard of gray solid for sashing

⅝ yard of gray stripe for binding

3¾ yards of fabric for backing

66" × 66" piece of batting

choosing fabrics

To create the checkerboard effect, first choose a fabric with a red background for the dark segments. For the lighter portions of the checkerboard, choose a print with a white background, but make sure there's plenty of red in the print. Small-scale prints work well.

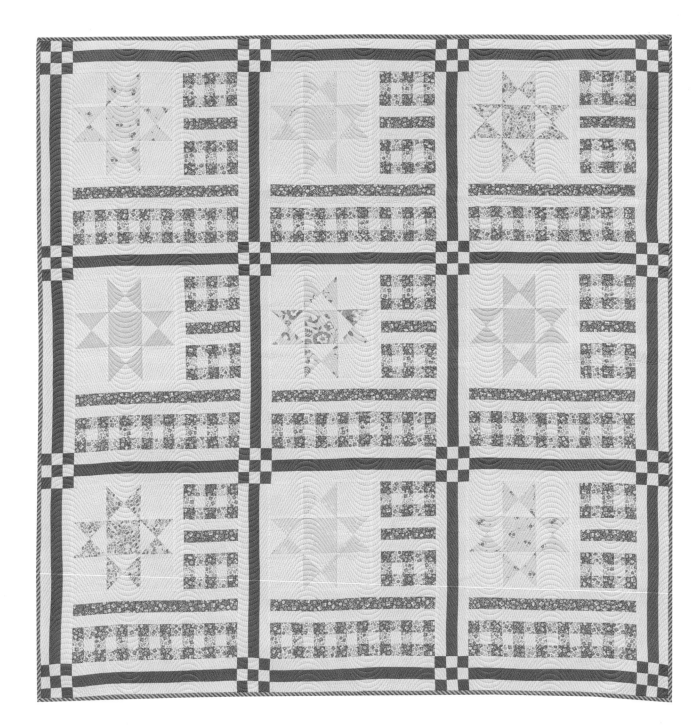

checkered flag

Designed by Corey Yoder
Pieced by Stephanie Crabtree
Quilted by Kaylene Parry

cutting

All measurements include ¼"-wide seam allowances.

From the red print, cut:

17 strips, 1½" × 42"; crosscut *7 of the strips* into:

- 9 strips, 1½" × 15½"
- 9 rectangles, 1½" × 5½"

From the white-and-red print, cut:

13 strips, 1½" × 42"

From the white solid, cut:

45 strips, 1½" × 42"; crosscut *15 of the strips* into:

- 18 strips, 1½" × 15½"
- 9 rectangles, 1½" × 9½"
- 18 rectangles, 1½" × 5½"

3 strips, 4½" × 42"; crosscut into 18 squares, 4½" × 4½"

4 strips, 3½" × 42"; crosscut into 36 squares, 3½" × 3½"

From *each* blue print, cut:

4 squares, 4½" × 4½" (20 total; 2 are extra)

2 squares, 3½" × 3½" (10 total; 1 is extra)

From the gray solid, cut:

16 strips, 1½" × 42"

From the gray stripe, cut:

7 strips, 2½" × 42"

making the checkerboard units

Press all seam allowances as indicated by the arrows.

1 Sew together two red 1½" × 42" strips and one white-and-red print 1½" × 42" strip as shown to make strip set A. Repeat to make a total of five strip sets. Crosscut the strip sets into 126 A segments measuring 1½" × 3½", including seam allowances.

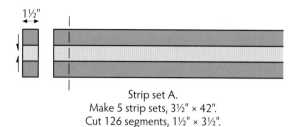

Strip set A.
Make 5 strip sets, 3½" × 42".
Cut 126 segments, 1½" × 3½".

2 Repeat step 1 using two white-and-red print 1½" × 42" strips and one white 1½" × 42" strip to make strip set B. Repeat to make a total of four B strip sets. Crosscut the strip sets into 99 B segments measuring 1½" × 3½", including seam allowances.

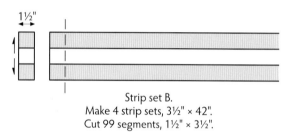

Strip set B.
Make 4 strip sets, 3½" × 42".
Cut 99 segments, 1½" × 3½".

3 Sew together three A segments and two B segments to make unit 1. Repeat to make a total of 18 units measuring 3½" × 5½", including seam allowances.

Unit 1.
Make 18 units,
3½" × 5½".

7 Sew a unit 1 to each long edge of a unit 3. Make a total of nine short checkerboard units measuring 5½" × 9½", including seam allowances.

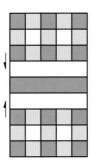

Make 9 short checkerboard units,
5½" × 9½".

8 Sew together a unit 2 and a unit 4. Make a total of nine long checkerboard units measuring 6½" × 15½", including seam allowances.

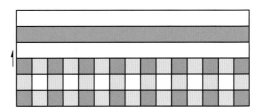

Make 9 long checkerboard units,
6½" × 15½".

making the star units

1 Select two white 4½" squares and two matching blue 4½" squares. Draw a diagonal line from corner to corner on the wrong side of each white square. Layer a marked square on top of each blue square, right sides together. Sew ¼" from both sides of the marked lines. Cut the units apart on the marked lines to make four half-square-triangle units. Do not worry about squaring these up just yet.

Make 4 units.

4 Sew together eight A segments and seven B segments to make unit 2. Make a total of nine units measuring 3½" × 15½", including seam allowances.

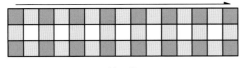

Unit 2.
Make 9 units, 3½" × 15½".

5 Sew a white 1½" × 5½" rectangle to each long edge of a red 1½" × 5½" rectangle to make unit 3. Make a total of nine units measuring 3½" × 5½", including seam allowances.

Unit 3.
Make 9 units, 3½" × 5½".

6 Sew a white 1½" × 15½" strip to each long edge of a red 1½" × 15½" strip to make unit 4. Make a total of nine units measuring 3½" × 15½", including seam allowances.

Unit 4.
Make 9 units, 3½" × 15½".

2 Draw a diagonal line from corner to corner and perpendicular to the seam on the wrong side of two of the half-square-triangle units. With the seams nested and the colors opposing each other, layer the marked units on top of the remaining two half-square-triangle units. Sew ¼" from both sides of the marked lines. Cut the units apart on the marked lines to make four quarter-square-triangle units. Trim each unit to 3½" square, including seam allowances. The center point of each quarter-square triangle will be 1¾" from each side.

Make 4 units.

3 Sew together the four matching quarter-square triangles, a matching blue print 3½" square, and four white 3½" squares to make a star unit measuring 9½" square, including seam allowances.

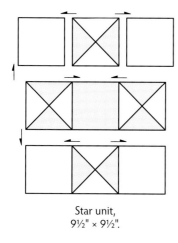

Star unit,
9½" × 9½".

4 Repeat steps 1–3 to make a total of nine star units, two from *each* of four blue prints and one from a different blue print. There will be two blue 4½" squares and one blue 3½" square left over.

assembling the blocks

1 Sew together one star unit, one white 1½" × 9½" rectangle, and one short checkerboard unit to make a block-top unit measuring 9½" × 15½", including seam allowances.

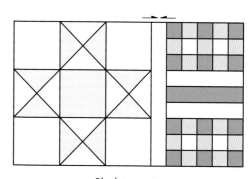

Block-top unit,
9½" × 15½".

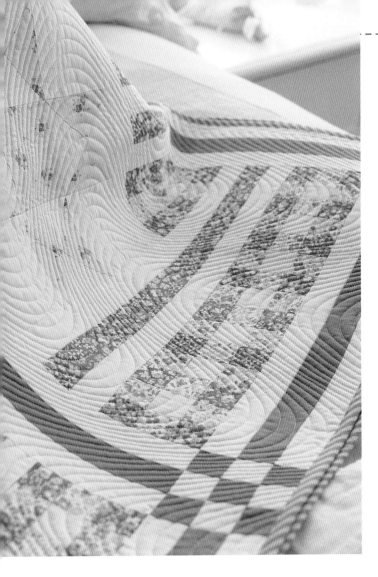

making the sashing

1. Sew together two white 1½" × 42" strips and one gray 1½" × 42" strip to make strip set C. Make 12 strip sets. Crosscut the strip sets into 24 segments measuring 3½" × 15½", including seam allowances, and 16 segments measuring 1½" × 3½", including seam allowances.

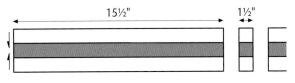

Strip set C.
Make 12 strip sets, 3½" × 42".
Cut 24 segments, 3½" × 15½", and 16 segments, 1½" × 3½".

2. Sew together two gray 1½" × 42" strips and one white 1½" × 42" strip to make strip set D. Make two strip sets. Crosscut the strip sets into 32 segments measuring 1½" × 3½", including seam allowances.

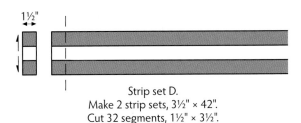

Strip set D.
Make 2 strip sets, 3½" × 42".
Cut 32 segments, 1½" × 3½".

3. Sew together one 1½" × 3½" C segment and two D segments to make a sashing cornerstone unit. Repeat to make a total of 16 units measuring 3½" square, including seam allowances.

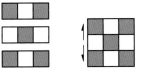

Make 16 cornerstone units,
3½" × 3½".

2. Sew a long checkerboard unit to the bottom of the block-top unit to make a Checkered Flag block. Make nine blocks measuring 15½" square, including seam allowances.

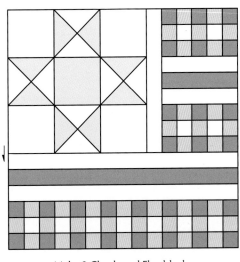

Make 9 Checkered Flag blocks,
15½" × 15½".

assembling the quilt top

1   Refer to the quilt assembly diagram below to arrange the sashing cornerstones and 12 of the 3½" × 15½" C sashing segments into four sashing rows. Sew together the pieces in each row.

2   Arrange the blocks and the 12 remaining 3½" × 15½" C sashing segments into three block rows. Sew together the pieces in each row.

3   Join the rows. The quilt top should measure 57½" square.

finishing the quilt

For help with any of the finishing steps, go to ShopMartingale.com/HowtoQuilt.

1   Layer the backing, batting, and quilt top; baste the layers together. Hand or machine quilt as desired. The quilt shown is machine quilted with an allover pattern of waves using the Modern Serpentine quilting design by Anita Shackelford.

2   Trim the excess batting and backing. Use the gray stripe 2½"-wide strips to make the binding. Attach the binding to the quilt.

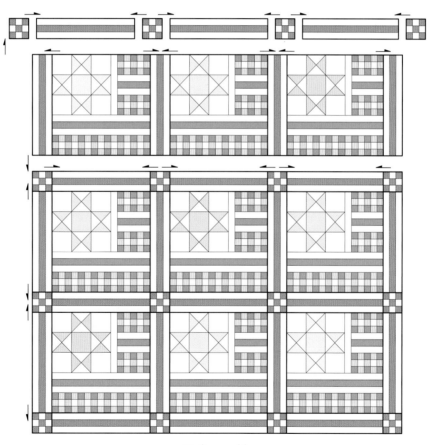

Quilt assembly

checkpoint

If you're like me, you have fabrics set aside that you're itching to work with, but you're just waiting to find the right project. When I saw Boro Wovens, I knew that I must use them. Checkpoint is the ideal design for two special fabrics that have been calling to you from your stash—or from your local quilt shop!

finished quilt: 57¼" × 57¼"
finished blocks: 8" × 8"

materials

Yardage is based on 42"-wide fabric. Fabrics for the quilt top are Boro Wovens, and binding fabric is from my Flower Mill collection, all from Moda Fabrics.

1⅓ yards of dark gray print for blocks

1⅝ yards of light gray print for blocks

2⅝ yards of white solid for blocks and setting triangles

⅝ yard of gray stripe for binding

3¾ yards of fabric for backing

66" × 66" piece of batting

choosing fabrics

If you're unfamiliar with woven fabrics like the Boro Wovens line, the design is created by weaving dyed threads rather than by printing dyes on the surface of the fabric. To create a checkerboard effect of woven threads in your quilt, choose a dark fabric and a light fabric of the same color. You'll want to use fabrics with small-scale motifs due to the small pieces in the design.

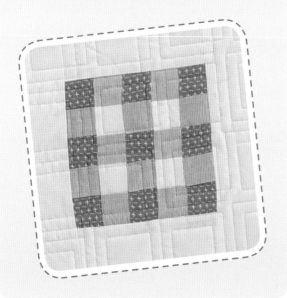

checkpoint

Designed by Corey Yoder
Pieced by Alyce Taylor
Quilted by Kaylene Parry

cutting

All measurements include ¼"-wide seam allowances.

From the dark gray print, cut:

18 strips, 1½" × 42"; crosscut *12 of the strips* into:
- 26 rectangles, 1½" × 8½"
- 26 rectangles, 1½" × 6½"

8 strips, 2" × 42"; crosscut into:
- 52 rectangles, 2" × 3½"
- 52 squares, 2" × 2"

From the light gray print, cut:

21 strips, 1½" × 42"; crosscut *14 of the strips* into:
- 32 rectangles, 1½" × 8½"
- 32 rectangles, 1½" × 6½"

10 strips, 2" × 42"; crosscut into:
- 64 rectangles, 2" × 3½"
- 64 squares, 2" × 2"

From the white solid, cut:

2 strips, 1½" × 42"

22 strips, 2" × 42"; crosscut into:
- 24 rectangles, 2" × 8½"
- 24 rectangles, 2" × 5½"
- 232 squares, 2" × 2"

3 strips, 3½" × 42"; crosscut into 29 squares, 3½" × 3½"

2 strips, 12⅝" × 42"; crosscut into:
- 4 squares, 12⅝" × 12⅝"; cut each square into quarters diagonally to yield 16 quarter-square triangles
- 2 squares, 6⅝" × 6⅝"; cut each square in half diagonally to yield 4 half-square triangles

From the gray stripe, cut:

7 strips, 2½" × 42"

making the checkerboard blocks

Press all seam allowances as indicated by the arrows.

1 Sew together three dark gray 1½" × 42" strips and two light gray 1½" × 42" strips to make strip set A. Make two strip sets. Crosscut the strip sets into 36 A segments measuring 1½" × 5½", including seam allowances.

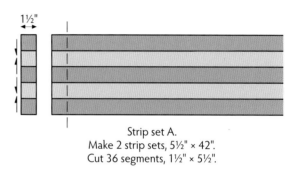

Strip set A.
Make 2 strip sets, 5½" × 42".
Cut 36 segments, 1½" × 5½".

2 Repeat step 1 using three light gray 1½" × 42" strips and two white 1½" × 42" strips to make strip set B. Crosscut the strip set into 24 B segments measuring 1½" × 5½", including seam allowances.

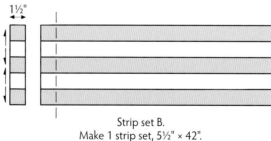

Strip set B.
Make 1 strip set, 5½" × 42".
Cut 24 segments, 1½" × 5½".

3 Sew together three A segments and two B segments to make a checkerboard unit. Make 12 checkerboard units measuring 5½" square, including seam allowances.

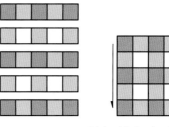

Make 12 checkerboard units, 5½" × 5½".

4 Sew white 2" × 5½" rectangles to the sides of a checkerboard unit. Sew white 2" × 8½" rectangles to the top and bottom of the unit to complete a Checkerboard block. Make 12 blocks measuring 8½" square, including seam allowances.

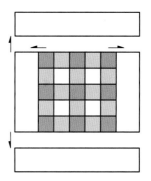

Make 12 Checkerboard blocks, 8½" × 8½".

making the star blocks

1 Draw a diagonal line from corner to corner on the wrong side of each white 2" square.

2 Place one marked 2" square right sides together on one end of a dark gray 2" × 3½" rectangle. Sew on the diagonal line. Trim the excess corner fabric, leaving a ¼" seam allowance. Repeat on the other end of the rectangle to make

a flying-geese unit. Repeat to make a total of 52 units measuring 2" × 3½", including seam allowances.

Make 52 units,
2" × 3½".

3 Sew together four flying-geese units, four dark gray 2" squares, and one white 3½" square to make a star unit. Make 13 star units measuring 6½" square, including seam allowances.

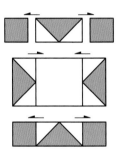 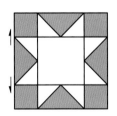

Make 13 star units,
6½" × 6½".

4 Sew dark gray 1½" × 6½" rectangles to the sides of a star unit. Sew dark gray 1½" × 8½" rectangles to the top and bottom of the unit to complete a dark gray Star block. Repeat to make a total of 13 dark gray Star blocks measuring 8½" square, including seam allowances.

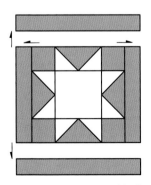

Make 13 dark gray Star blocks,
8½" × 8½".

5 Repeat steps 2–4 to make 16 light gray Star blocks, substituting light gray pieces for the dark gray pieces.

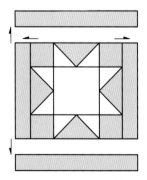

Make 16 light gray Star blocks,
8½" × 8½".

assembling the quilt top

Refer to the quilt assembly diagram below to arrange the blocks and white setting triangles in diagonal rows as shown. Sew together the pieces in each row. Join the rows. Add the corner triangles last. The quilt top should measure 57¼" square.

finishing the quilt

For help with any of the finishing steps, go to ShopMartingale.com/HowtoQuilt.

1   Layer the backing, batting, and quilt top; baste the layers together. Hand or machine quilt as desired. The quilt shown is machine quilted with an allover pattern of diamonds using the Diagonal Plaid quilting design by Patricia E. Ritter.

2   Trim the excess batting and backing. Use the gray stripe 2½"-wide strips to make the binding. Attach the binding to the quilt.

Quilt assembly

maple leaf check

Welcome cooler autumn days with a design that seems to flutter like falling leaves. Each leaf in Maple Leaf Check uses half-square triangles, and sometimes triangles can feel a little intimidating—but they don't need to be. See "Trimming Triangles" on page 43 and watch every leaf in your quilt fall beautifully into place.

finished quilt: 58½" × 70½"
finished blocks: 10" × 10"

materials

Yardage is based on 42"-wide fabric. Fabrics for the quilt top are from my various collections, and binding fabric is from my Canning Day collection, all from Moda Fabrics.

½ yard *each* of dark coral, dark gray, dark green, dark red, and dark yellow prints for blocks (collectively referred to as "dark")

¼ yard *each* of light coral, light gray, light green, light red, and light yellow prints for blocks (collectively referred to as "light")

¼ yard of gray print for sashing cornerstones

4 yards of white solid for blocks and sashing

⅝ yard of gray stripe for binding

3¾ yards of fabric for backing

67" × 79" piece of batting

choosing fabrics

Even though this is a fall quilt, don't assume the fabrics must be fall themed. It's the colors of the fabric that will make the most impact. Choose your favorite colors for fall and soon you'll be "falling" in love with your new quilt.

cutting

All measurements include ¼"-wide seam allowances.

From *each* dark print, cut:

1 strip, 4½" × 42"; crosscut into 6 squares, 4½" × 4½" (30 total)

2 strips, 3" × 42"; crosscut into 18 squares, 3" × 3" (90 total)

2 strips, 2½" × 42"; crosscut into 24 squares, 2½" × 2½" (120 total)

From *each* light print, cut:

1 strip, 3" × 42"; crosscut into 12 squares, 3" × 3" (60 total)

1 strip, 2½" × 42"; crosscut into 12 squares, 2½" × 2½" (60 total)

From the gray print, cut:

2 strips, 2½" × 42"; crosscut into 20 squares, 2½" × 2½"

From the white solid, cut:

6 strips, 4" × 42"; crosscut into 60 squares, 4" × 4"

12 strips, 3" × 42"; crosscut into 150 squares, 3" × 3"

27 strips, 2½" × 42"; crosscut into:
- 49 rectangles, 2½" × 10½"
- 150 squares, 2½" × 2½"

From the gray stripe, cut:

7 strips, 2½" × 42"

maple leaf check

Designed by Corey Yoder
Pieced by Sherry McConnell
Quilted by Kaylene Parry

making the blocks

Press all seam allowances as indicated by the arrows. The instructions are written for making one block at a time. For each block you will need the following pieces:

A matching set of:
- 3 dark 3" squares
- 1 dark 4½" square
- 4 dark 2½" squares

In the same colorway as the dark print, a matching set of:
- 2 light 3" squares
- 2 light 2½" squares

1   Draw a diagonal line from corner to corner on the wrong side of five white 3" squares.

2   Layer three marked squares on top of the dark 3" squares, right sides together. Sew ¼" from both sides of the marked lines. Cut the units apart on the marked lines to make six dark half-square-triangle units. Trim each unit to 2½" square, including seam allowances.

Make 6 dark units.

3   Repeat step 2 with the remaining marked squares and two light 3" squares to make four light half-square-triangle units.

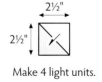

Make 4 light units.

4 Draw a diagonal line from corner to corner on the wrong side of two white 4" squares. Layer one marked square on the upper-right corner of a dark 4½" square. Sew on the marked line. Trim the excess corner fabric, leaving a ¼" seam allowance. Repeat on the opposite corner to make a stem unit measuring 4½" square, including seam allowances.

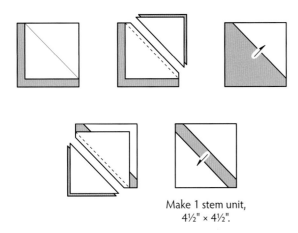

Make 1 stem unit,
4½" × 4½".

5 Arrange two white 2½" squares, two dark half-square-triangle units, one light half-square-triangle unit, and one dark 2½" square in two rows. Sew together the pieces in each row. Join the rows. Sew the stem unit to the right edge to make a unit measuring 4½" × 10½", including seam allowances.

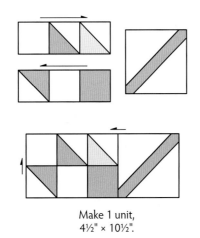

Make 1 unit,
4½" × 10½".

6 Arrange three white, two light, and three dark 2½" squares, and the remaining light and dark half-square-triangle units into three vertical rows. Sew together the pieces in each row. Join the rows. Sew the unit from step 5 to the right edge to make one block measuring 10½" square, including seam allowances.

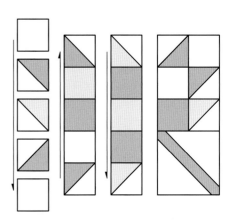

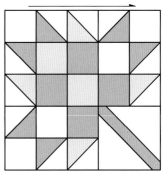

Make 1 Leaf block,
10½" × 10½".

7 Repeat steps 1–6 to make 6 blocks from each color family (30 blocks total).

assembling the quilt top

1 Refer to the quilt assembly diagram below to join five blocks and four white 2½" × 10½" rectangles to make a block row. Make six block rows measuring 10½" × 58½", including seam allowances.

2 Join five white 2½" × 10½" rectangles and four gray 2½" squares to make a sashing row. Make five sashing rows measuring 2½" × 58½", including seam allowances.

3 Join the block rows and sashing rows. The quilt top should measure 58½" × 70½".

finishing the quilt

For help with any of the finishing steps, go to ShopMartingale.com/HowtoQuilt.

1 Layer the backing, batting, and quilt top; baste the layers together. Hand or machine quilt as desired. The quilt shown is machine quilted with an allover pattern resembling blowing leaves using the Frozen Swirls quilting design by Anne Bright.

2 Trim the excess batting and backing. Use the gray stripe 2½"-wide strips to make the binding. Attach the binding to the quilt.

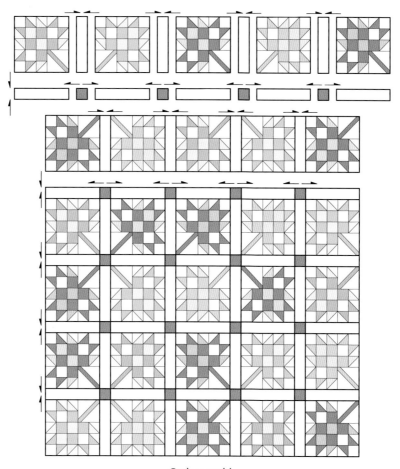

Quilt assembly

checking it twice

If you've been making a quilter's wish list and checking it twice, you know that a new quilt for Christmas would be nice! For a festive design that's full of holiday cheer, gather up some red and green fabrics and let them all play together on a field of snowy white.

finished quilt: 68" × 81½"
finished blocks: 13½" × 13½"

materials

Yardage is based on 42"-wide fabric. Fat quarters measure 18" × 21". Fabrics for the quilt top are from various collections, and the binding fabric is from my Flower Mill collection, all from Moda Fabrics.

15 fat quarters of assorted red prints for blocks

15 fat quarters of assorted green prints for blocks

4 yards of white solid for blocks

⅝ yard of red stripe for binding

5⅜ yards of fabric for backing

76" × 89" piece of batting

choosing fabrics

When selecting fabrics for Checking It Twice, look for small-scale prints. Half of the fabrics should have a red background, and half should have a green background.

checking it twice

Designed by Corey Yoder
Pieced by Stephanie Crabtree
Quilted by Kaylene Parry

cutting

All measurements include ¼"-wide seam allowances. See the fat-quarter cutting guide below to cut the pieces from each red and green print.

From *each* red and green print, cut:

1 strip, 2" × 18" (15 red and 15 green total)

8 squares, 3½" × 3½" (120 red and 120 green total)

5 rectangles, 2" × 7" (75 red and 75 green total)

3 rectangles, 2" × 5" (45 red and 45 green total)

From the white solid, cut:

24 strips, 3½" × 42"; crosscut into 120 rectangles, 3½" × 8"

23 strips, 2" × 42"; crosscut into:
- 30 strips, 2" × 18"
- 60 rectangles, 2" × 5"

From the red stripe, cut:

8 strips, 2½" × 42"

making the blocks

Press all seam allowances as indicated by the arrows. The instructions are written for making one block at a time. For each block you will need the following pieces:

A matching set of:
- 1 red 2" × 18" strip
- 8 red 3½" squares

From a different print, a matching set of:
- 3 red 2" × 7" rectangles

A matching set of:
- 2 green 2" × 7" rectangles
- 3 green 2" × 5" rectangles

1 Sew together the red 2" × 18" strip and one white 2" × 18" strip to make a strip set. Crosscut the strip set into eight segments measuring 2" × 3½", including seam allowances.

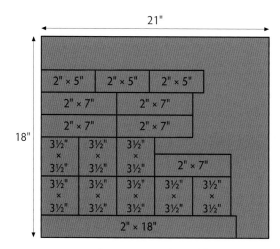

Fat-quarter cutting guide

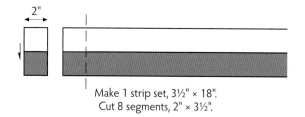

Make 1 strip set, 3½" × 18".
Cut 8 segments, 2" × 3½".

2 Sew together two segments to create a four-patch unit measuring 3½" square, including seam allowances. Make four.

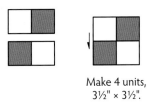

Make 4 units,
3½" × 3½".

3 Draw a diagonal line from corner to corner on the wrong side of the red 3½" squares. Place one marked square right sides together on one end of a white 3½" × 8" rectangle. Sew on the marked line. Refer to "Flip the Flying Geese," right, to trim the excess corner fabric, leaving a ¼" seam allowance. Repeat on the other end to make a flying-geese unit. Make four units measuring 3½" × 8", including seam allowances.

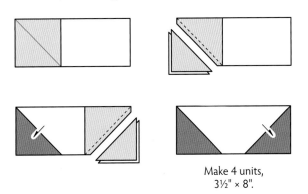

Make 4 units,
3½" × 8".

4 Sew together three red 2" × 7" rectangles and two green 2" × 7" rectangles to make a strip set. Crosscut the strip set into three segments measuring 2" × 8", including seam allowances.

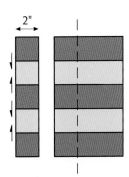

Make 1 strip set, 7" × 8".
Cut 3 segments, 2" × 8".

5 Repeat step 4 using three green 2" × 5" rectangles and two white 2" × 5" rectangles. Crosscut the strip set into two segments measuring 2" × 8", including seam allowances.

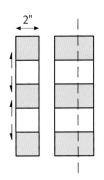

Make 1 strip set, 5" × 8".
Cut 2 segments, 2" × 8".

flip the flying geese

I've got a nifty trick for making flying-geese units using the stitch-and-flip method. After sewing on the marked diagonal line, I press the seam allowance of the upper square over before trimming the bottom two layers. All edges should line up nicely, with no part of the top square extending beyond the edges of the bottom pieces. If my sewing isn't as accurate as I would like, I can easily correct it because nothing has been trimmed away.

6 Sew together the step 4 and step 5 segments to make one checkerboard unit measuring 8" square.

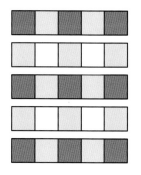 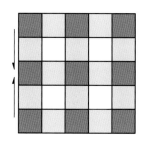

Make 1 checkerboard unit, 8" × 8".

7 Sew together the four-patch units, the flying-geese units, and the checkerboard unit to make a red Star block measuring 14" square, including seam allowances. Repeat to make a total of 15 red Star blocks.

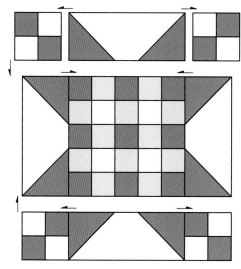

Make 15 red Star blocks, 14" × 14".

8 Repeat steps 1–7 to make a total of 15 green Star blocks using the following red and green pieces for each block:

A matching set of:
- 1 green 2" × 18" strip
- 8 green 3½" squares

From a different print, a matching set of:
- 3 green 2" × 7" rectangles

A matching set of:
- 2 red 2" × 7" rectangles
- 3 red 2" × 5" rectangles

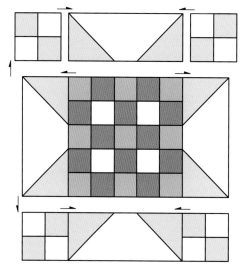

Make 15 green Star blocks, 14" × 14".

assembling the quilt top

1 Refer to the quilt assembly diagram below to arrange the blocks in six horizontal rows of five blocks each. Sew together the blocks in each row.

2 Join the rows. The quilt top should measure 68" × 81½".

finishing the quilt

For help with any of the finishing steps, go to ShopMartingale.com/HowtoQuilt.

1 Layer the backing, batting, and quilt top; baste the layers together. Hand or machine quilt as desired. The quilt shown is machine quilted with an allover pattern resembling snowflakes using the Razzle Dazzle Down quilting design by Julie Hirt. It adds a perfect festive touch.

2 Trim the excess batting and backing. Use the red stripe 2½"-wide strips to make the binding. Attach the binding to the quilt.

Quilt assembly

coat check

What a fun, fresh look you can create with a large-scale gingham design surrounded by smaller checks in the border. Generous 12"-square blocks give each snowman the perfect place to perch and enjoy the wintry view. When the weather outside is frightful, make a quilt that's completely delightful!

finished quilt: 72½" × 72½"
finished snowman block: 12" × 12"
finished border block: 6" × 6"

materials

Yardage is based on 42"-wide fabric. Fabrics for the quilt top and binding are from Sweet Tea by Sweetwater from Moda Fabrics.

2 yards of light blue print for blocks and border

2⅓ yards of dark blue print for blocks and border

4⅛ yards of white solid for blocks and border

⅛ yard of orange solid for carrot noses

⅝ yard of navy stripe for binding

4⅝ yards of fabric for backing

81" × 81" piece of batting

¼ yard of 17"-wide lightweight paper-backed fusible web

6½" square acrylic ruler (optional)

choosing fabrics

When selecting fabrics for Coat Check, choose a dark print and a light print in the same color. For a cohesive look, I picked a dark blue and a light blue with the same print.

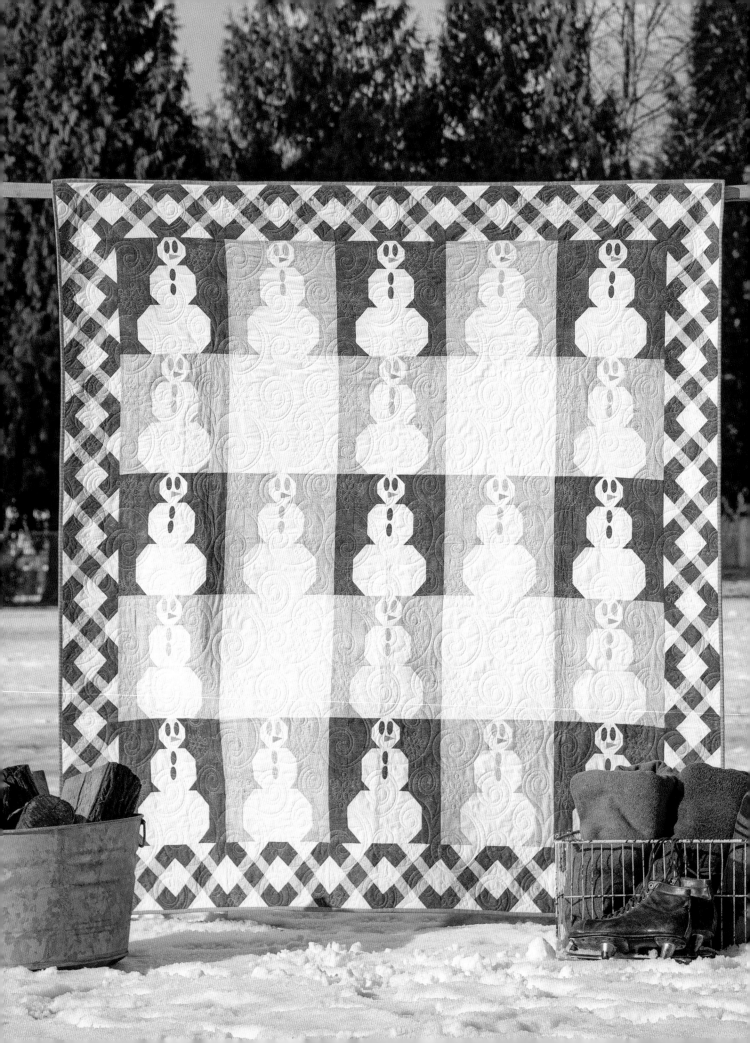

cutting

All measurements include ¼"-wide seam allowances.

From the light blue print, cut:

3 strips, 3" × 42"; crosscut into 24 rectangles, 3" × 3½"

8 strips, 2½" × 42"; crosscut into 24 rectangles, 2½" × 12½"

6 strips, 2" × 42"; crosscut into:
- 24 rectangles, 2" × 4½"
- 48 squares, 2" × 2"

15 strips, 1½" × 42"; crosscut into:
- 176 rectangles, 1½" × 2¼"
- 96 squares, 1½" × 1½"

From the dark blue print, cut:

2 strips, 3" × 42"; crosscut into 18 rectangles, 3" × 3½"

6 strips, 2½" × 42"; crosscut into 18 rectangles, 2½" × 12½"

18 strips, 2¼" × 42"; crosscut into:
- 176 rectangles, 2¼" × 3¼"
- 44 squares, 2¼" × 2¼"

5 strips, 2" × 42"; crosscut into:
- 18 rectangles, 2" × 4½"
- 36 squares, 2" × 2"

3 strips, 1½" × 42"; crosscut into 72 squares, 1½" × 1½"

From the white solid, cut:

2 strips, 12½" × 42"; crosscut into 4 squares, 12½" × 12½"

6 strips, 5½" × 42"; crosscut into 21 rectangles, 5½" × 8½"

3 strips, 4½" × 42"; crosscut into 21 rectangles, 4½" × 5½"

18 strips, 3½" × 42"; crosscut into 197 squares, 3½" × 3½"

From the navy stripe, cut:

8 strips, 2½" × 42"

making the snowman blocks

Press all seam allowances as indicated by the arrows.

1 Draw a diagonal line from corner to corner on the wrong side of 48 light blue 1½" squares. Place a marked square on a corner of a white 3½" square, right sides together. Sew on the marked line. Trim the excess corner fabric, leaving a ¼" seam allowance. Repeat on the remaining three corners. Sew light blue 3" × 3½" rectangles to the sides to make unit 1. Make a total of 12 units measuring 3½" × 8½", including seam allowances.

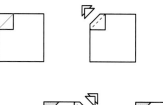

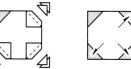

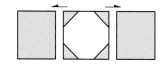

Unit 1.
Make 12 units,
3½" × 8½".

coat check

Designed by Corey Yoder
Pieced by Christy Bowman
Quilted by Kaylene Parry

2   Repeat step 1 using light blue 1½" squares, a white 4½" × 5½" rectangle, and light blue 2" × 4½" rectangles to make unit 2. Make a total of 12 units measuring 4½" × 8½", including seam allowances.

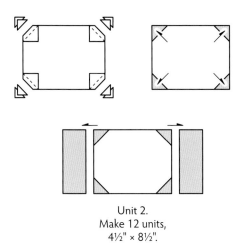

Unit 2.
Make 12 units,
4½" × 8½".

3   Repeat step 1 using light blue 2" squares and a white 5½" × 8½" rectangle to make unit 3. Make a total of 12 units measuring 5½" × 8½", including seam allowances.

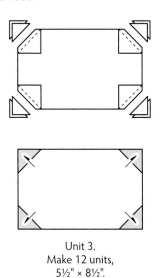

Unit 3.
Make 12 units,
5½" × 8½".

4   Sew together one each of units 1–3. Sew a light blue 2½" × 12½" rectangle to each side to make a Snowman block. Repeat to make a total of 12 light blue Snowman blocks measuring 12½" square, including seam allowances.

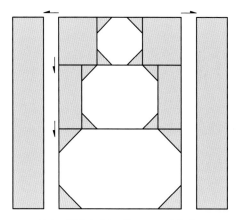

Make 12 light blue Snowman blocks,
12½" × 12½".

5   Repeat steps 1–4 to make nine dark blue Snowman blocks, substituting dark blue pieces for the light blue pieces.

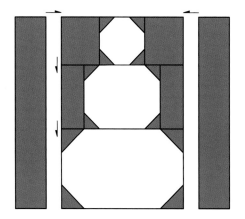

Make 9 dark blue Snowman blocks,
12½" × 12½".

appliquéing the snowman blocks

1 Use the oval template pattern on page 63 to trace 84 ovals onto the paper side of the fusible web. Use the carrot template to trace 21 carrots onto the paper side of the fusible web. Cut out, leaving approximately ⅛" around the perimeter of each shape.

2 Following the guidelines for your fusible web, fuse 48 ovals onto the wrong side of a piece of the light blue print and 36 ovals onto the wrong side of a piece of the dark blue print. Fuse 21 carrots onto the wrong side of the orange solid. Cut out each shape on the marked line and remove the paper.

3 Refer to the appliqué placement guide to arrange and fuse the shapes on each snowman using the recommended heat settings for the fusible web you're using.

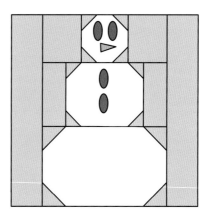

Appliqué placement

4 Use a straight stitch to machine appliqué the shapes in place.

making the border blocks

1 Sew together one dark blue 2¼" × 3¼" rectangle and one light blue 1½" × 2¼" rectangle. Repeat to make a total of 176 units measuring 2½" × 5", including seam allowances.

Make 176 units, 2½" × 5".

2 Sew together four step 1 units, one dark blue 2¼" square, and four white 3½" squares. Note that the white squares are not even with the perimeter of the block. Doing so will reduce the amount of fabric you'll be trimming away in step 3. Repeat to make a total of 44 units.

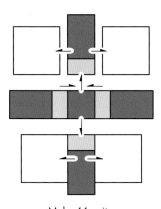

Make 44 units.

3 See "Handle with Care" below left and use the 6½" square ruler (optional) to trim the units to 6½" square, including seam allowances. Repeat to make a total of 44 border blocks.

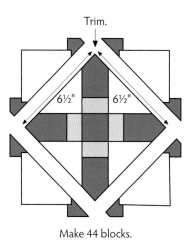

Trim.

6½" 6½"

Make 44 blocks.

handle with care

Be careful when piecing the border squares. Because of the way they're constructed, the blocks will be on the bias after trimming, which means they'll stretch more than most quilt blocks. Try not to pull on them when piecing or ironing, because they can stretch out of shape.

assembling the quilt top

1 Refer to the quilt assembly diagram to arrange the Snowman blocks and white 12½" squares in five horizontal rows of five pieces each. Sew together the blocks and squares in each row. Join the rows. The quilt center should measure 60½" square, including seam allowances.

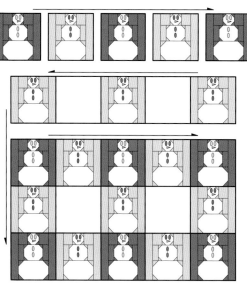

Quilt assembly

2 Sew together 10 border blocks to make each of the side borders. Sew the borders to the sides of the quilt.

3 Sew together 12 border blocks to make each of the top/bottom borders. Sew the borders to the top and bottom of the quilt. The quilt top should measure 72½" square.

Adding borders

finishing the quilt

For help with any of the finishing steps, go to ShopMartingale.com/HowtoQuilt.

1 Layer the backing, batting, and quilt top; baste the layers together. Hand or machine quilt as desired. The quilt shown is machine quilted with an allover pattern of swirls and snowflakes using the First Snow quilting design by Anne Bright.

2 Trim the excess batting and backing. Use the navy stripe 2½"-wide strips to prepare the binding. Attach the binding to the quilt.

Oval
Cut 36 from dark blue print
and 48 from light blue print.

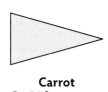

Carrot
Cut 21 from orange.

cute as a button

If appliqué isn't your favorite, this quilt would be adorable if you substituted actual buttons for the appliquéd buttons and for the eyes. Opt to skip the carrot noses and purchase carrot-shaped buttons instead.

about the author

Corey Yoder

I grew up in and still reside in a small Amish community in Ohio. I come from a line of quilters on both sides of my family and have been surrounded by quilts and fabric my entire life. Quilts were always in the frame waiting to be hand quilted. Quilt get-togethers always meant much laughter and good food, and perhaps playing with cousins under the quilt frame.

After I married my husband, Ryan, in 1997 at the age of 19, my love of fabric blossomed. I hadn't sewn while living at home, despite my mother's best attempts, but I dived into buying fabric without knowing what I would do with it. We've probably all been there— walking into a quilt shop with all of the sights and smells of fabrics, knowing that some of it will be going home with us! It seemed natural to turn my fabric purchases into a quilt, and one quilt quickly led to two and has now turned into hundreds.

I began designing quilts in 2010, and my work has since been featured in many quilting magazines and books. My first book, *Playful Petals*, was published in 2014. I began designing fabric for Moda Fabrics the following year and launched my quilt-pattern business, Coriander Quilts (Corey and her quilts), at the same time.

The comment I hear most about my fabrics is, "Your fabrics make me feel happy." I wholeheartedly embrace the idea that quilts and fabric should always bring joy and spread love. I am so thankful for the wonderful quilting community I have met in person as well as those I know online. Your support of my patterns and fabrics means that I get to keep doing what I love. Thank you!

For more about my patterns and fabrics, visit CorianderQuilts.com.